LANNY PARKS

ALSO BY JAN DE HARTOG

BOOKS

The Outer Buoy: A Story of the Ultimate Voyage

The Peculiar People

The Centurion

The Commodore

Star of Peace

The Trail of the Serpent

The Lamb's War

The Peaceable Kingdom

The Children

The Captain

The Call of the Sea
(including *The Lost Sea*, *The Distant Shore*, *A Sailor's Life*)

The Hospital

The Artist

Waters of the New World: Houston to Nantucket

The Inspector

The Spiral Road

A Sailor's Life

The Little Ark

The Distant Shore
(composed of "Stella" and "Thalassa")

The Lost Sea

Captain Jan
(translated from the Dutch "Hollands Glorie")

PLAYS

William and Mary

The Fourposter

Skipper Next to God

This Time Tomorrow

A VIEW OF THE OCEAN

JAN DE HARTOG

A VIEW

OF THE OCEAN

PANTHEON BOOKS, NEW YORK

Library of Congress Cataloging-in-Publication Data

De Hartog, Jan, 1914–2002.
A view of the ocean / Jan de Hartog.
p.   cm.
ISBN 978-0-375-42470-0
1. De Hartog, Jan, 1914–2002. 2. Authors, Dutch—20th
century—Biography. 3. Authors, English—20th century—
Biography. I. Title.
PT5838.H65Z46 2007   823'.914—dc22   [B]   2006102683

www.pantheonbooks.com

Printed in the United States of America
First Edition
2 4 6 8 9 7 5 3 1

I saw that there was an ocean of
darkness and death,
but an infinite ocean of light and
love flowed over the ocean of darkness.

—GEORGE FOX, 1647

A VIEW OF THE OCEAN

ONE

MY MOTHER DIED at the age of seventy-nine. She was a gentle, saintly woman who had always seemed somewhat intimidated by her husband and her two sons. My father was a giant of a man, a professor of theology at the University of Amsterdam and a famous Protestant pastor. He could be considered one of the last Victorians, as Holland, up to World War II, was a generation behind the times; social and philosophical problems that had obsessed the world at the turn of the century were still tackled with crusading fervor in Holland in 1925.

My parents first met in 1903 when she was in her early twenties and he was approaching forty. He was a big, swarthy bachelor, pastor of a hamlet in the backwoods of Holland, and one morning he went to visit his uncle—a more dignified clergyman in a neighboring town—riding a bicycle, a big floppy black hat on his head, an umbrella in two saber clamps on the front of the bicycle, and a roll of piano music on its carrier. My mother, as he described it to us later, was sitting in his uncle's orchard, underneath a flowering cherry tree, dressed in blue shantung with white lace cuffs and ruffs. Her burnished golden hair glowed in the sunlight, her blue eyes looked at him gravely, and he instantly realized that this was the woman he had been waiting for. Her version was that she was sitting reading underneath the solitary tree in the front garden of his uncle's vicarage when, suddenly, a huge man on a woman's bicycle came careening through the gate and skidded in the gravel, and for a heart-stopping moment she was afraid he was about to slam into her. Then he let himself fall sideways, which seemed to be the only way of alighting from his machine, came towards her, and said, "Good morning. I am Arnold de Hartog." He did not ask her who she was and she did not tell him; she instantly realized that he was a sweet, quasi-masterful man who was badly in need of care, with his frayed trouser cuffs, tangled hair, and dirty fingernails, which would not do at all for a clergyman.

They fell in love, became engaged, were married, moved to the city of Haarlem, and had one son. He upset the household profoundly, because my father did not like having someone else around to claim my mother's attention; my brother had a thin time of it until I arrived to help him out some years later. My father adored my mother passionately, wholeheartedly, totally, but his love claimed complete possession of the object of his adoration. He was at heart a simple man, bighearted, big-stomached, big-muscled, who might have turned into a brute if God had not dominated his life. He often said that, but for God, he would have become a pirate, or a general, or a teacher of gymnastics. He moved through life with the gusto and the commotion of a wagon train. The stories my mother told us later about our family vacations in those early years make them sound like troop movements.

Every summer we used to go to a hotel in Königswinter on the German Rhine for six weeks; I vaguely remember traveling there by paddle steamer. I remember the smell of German cooking and the tinkling sound of the trio that played during dinner; I remember the ruins of castles on high, somber rocks dominating the river. To go on vacation was not, in our case, a simple matter of moving to a hotel with a few suitcases; we had to bring along the things without which my father could not feel at home. These included a hip bath, a tea service, his own silverware, three footlockers full of books that he never looked at but had to have around because one never knew when inspiration might strike for a philosophical treatise. We also had to include, for a reason known only to him, a life-size plaster bust of the philosopher Schopenhauer.

One thing became obvious after two or three weeks: He was bored to tears in Königswinter. But each year he would book our rooms for six weeks, in advance. It came as a tremendous relief to everybody when we could make our way back to our own house, where he could relax at last, with his silverware, his tea service, his books, his plaster bust of Schopenhauer, to say nothing of the hip bath, which my brother and I remember vividly because of the hippopotamic sounds that came from the bathroom as my mother poured water over him and they both scrubbed away at his huge body with long-handled brushes.

I suppose it is a mystery to most children why their parents love each other. As we grew older, my brother and I occasionally discussed the enigma of our mother's devotion to this man. We never questioned his devotion to her; she was really a saintly woman, she had better be, for no one but a saint could have stood a lifetime shared with Arnold de Hartog. To us he seemed at times a monster of egocentricity, a tyrant, a blustering bully; to her he was always a sensitive, shy, and helpless man with a mission.

She believed in his mission from the first moment she saw him until the day he died, even until the day she herself died, some twenty years later. She was convinced that he had a message to give to the world, that his theological system was an innovation, a new and indispensable help to the understanding of the nature of God. Even so, she had to get away from him occasionally, if only for a little while, alone, to do some digging for her own soul. As wives of the period were not entitled to a yearly vacation like any other member of the free professions, she had only one way out: to fall ill. She was purported to have some mysterious gastrointestinal ailment that no doctor ever could quite diagnose; the recommended treatment was for her to lie flat on her back for a month in some serene surroundings every year or two. During that time, my father went out of his mind with grief and anxiety, a stumbling, whimpering colossus in a panic. He went to see her every day, with gifts of little works of art that I still remember clearly. We came across a hatbox full of them when we sorted out my mother's possessions after her death. They were useless, monstrous objets d'art, wooden boxes in unnatural shapes such as horses' hooves or pretzels, tiny vases for midget flowers, doll-sized household objects made of brass—milk jug, coal scuttle, miniature pots and pans. I remember that as a child, I longed to play with them, but Mother said, "No, no! Those are not toys! They are gifts from your father!" So all I could do was scowl at them.

Under the wings of her faith in him and her high opinion of his abilities as a philosopher, he became one. He wrote a treatise titled *Necessary Additions to Calvin's Institutes*, which caused some commotion in theological circles, as the treatise consisted of three volumes, whereas *Calvin's Institutes* consisted of one. He started a philosophical monthly called *New Pathways*, which he filled single-handedly with articles by "Doctor de Hartog," by "A. de H.," "A.," "H.," "de H.," and by "Ed." There also was a section for correspondence, which he managed to fill as well. I remember, for example, that he came downstairs from his study one day to lunch and asked my mother, busy cutting up his sandwiches into fingers for him, "Luc, would you ask me to explain the difference in the concept of free will according to Schopenhauer and according to Nietzsche?"

My mother looked up, frowning. "I beg your pardon?"

"Ask me," he repeated irritably, "what the difference is in the concept of free will between Schopenhauer and Nietzsche. Just *ask* me."

She said, "Why ask you? I know."

He cried, exasperated, "I know you know! But ask me!"

So she obediently asked, "Would you explain to me the difference in the concept of free will between Schopenhauer and Nietzsche?"

Then he said, "Excellent. Now, what's for lunch?"

That was the last we heard of it until the next issue of the monthly appeared. There, under the section "Correspondence," was a letter starting, *An intelligent reader asks: What is the difference in the concept of free will* . . . My father could not possibly have written his lengthy response without someone actually having asked the question. He was an honest man.

It was a persnickety honesty, in the eyes of us boys. We were too young to realize how important it was to someone with his nature to adhere to the absolute truth at all times. For he had a florid imagination; he loved, as Renoir put it, "to correct nature." Only by keeping a tight rein on himself could he stick to the truth, and this became, as it turned out, his most outstanding virtue. His philosophy my brother and I not only never understood, we never tried to understand it. His sermons, to which we were frequently taken—although, theoretically, we were left completely free—left no impression on us whatsoever. What we both remembered was his radiant honesty. He was a man who truly believed what he preached, and was at pains to practice it as much as possible. Nowadays, when "sincerity" is for sale on Madison Avenue, men like my father are remembered with nostalgia. Seen from our point of view, he lived in a better, cleaner world, where mankind could still claim some innocence. After the insane slaughter of youth in World War I, there was no innocence left in Western man. My father kept his for another twenty years because Holland was not involved in that conflict; we were neutral. I remember, as a boy, hearing distant thunder when we were on vacation; Königswinter came later, after the war, but in those early days we went to a small bathing resort in the Dutch province of Zeeland, across the Scheldt from Belgium. In the evening, when our family joined others in wicker beach chairs on the sandy banks of the estuary, we would hear a distant thunder, although the sky was clear, and someone would say, "Poor boys." What we heard were the guns of Flanders.

My father remained a confident, sincerely optimistic Victorian until the day he died; he died just before the Western world was once again engulfed by that murderous insanity. He knew about Hitler, and about the early persecution of the Jews, and while he could not visualize its nightmarish reality, he protested against it vigorously, together with the spiritual leaders of other nations, just as he protested against the execution of the Scottsboro boys in the United States and the imprisonment of Catholic missionaries in China. Secretly, I suspect, he had a sneaking admiration in those early days for the Wagnerian histrionics of Hitler and Mussolini. For although he preached with conviction about gentle Jesus, meek and mild, he opened his inaugural lecture at the University of Amsterdam with the ringing words "Christianity is heroism!" This was the cry with which he entered the academic ring to defend theology as an exact science. Later, to us, his sons, this cry came to sound strangely romantic and outmoded. My brother spent three years in Japanese prison camps and had his appendix removed by a fellow prisoner with a penknife without anesthetics. I lived through three years of German occupation and escaped to England through Occupied Europe. By the end of the war, we each had developed an aversion to the word "heroism." Until the end of his days, my father lived in the unshakable belief that Mankind was striding forcefully and purposefully ahead on the spiral road of evolution, led by Heroes, temporal and spiritual. His sons saw Mankind fall into a snake pit of murderous insanity, where the Sermon on the Mount was read aloud to bomber crews about to take off to obliterate Berlin. We had heard demagogues twist concepts and ideas around until they converged into the opposite of what they used to mean; we had seen the name

of God embossed on the buckles of the belts of the
Wehrmacht. If to be a Christian meant to be a Hero in
my father's harmless prewar world, then what was it
supposed to mean now? The only definitions that
remained, after all was said and done in the name of
God and His son, were either "crackpot" or "hypo-
crite." I, for one, would have dismissed the whole concept of God and His unholy trappings as just another of
mankind's delusions on its way to self-annihilation,
but for two seemingly irrelevant incidents in the past.

As a boy of ten, I had discovered, to my profound
amazement, that my father actually did believe in God.
Until then I had assumed that "God" was another
Santa Claus, to be used as a stick behind the door for
unruly children. My brother and I would wait during
grace at table for the stomach rumbles, in order to
burst into suppressed giggles; our father, despite his
tightly closed eyes and tightly folded hands, could never
keep his face straight. We assumed that the whole thing
was a convention, like manners: you had to wash hands
and you had to say grace; you had to pretend that you

enjoyed the visits of Aunt Clara and that you believed in God. If that made everybody happy, that was what you did.

One afternoon I was sent to mow the lawn. I was on my way, reluctantly, when I suddenly came upon my father praying alone behind the bicycle shed. He did not realize that he was being observed; he stood there, eyes closed, hands folded, face lifted, in what he obviously believed to be a private moment. I found myself forced to the astounding conclusion that God was real to him, that religion was not just a family convention.

The other incident took place in 1933, when I was nineteen and my brother was away in the Dutch East Indies. A big, popular rally had been organized in Amsterdam to protest against the first of the pogroms that the Nazis had organized against the Jews in Germany. The rally was to be in the Amsterdam Bicycle Hall, a vast covered stadium where bicycle races, automobile exhibitions, and tennis tournaments were held. Three speakers of different denominations were scheduled to speak: a rabbi, a Catholic priest, and a Protestant minister. The event was given a good deal of publicity, and public feeling about the pogrom in Germany was running high; it was likely that many people would turn out for it, their emotions at fever pitch. The Dutch Nazi Party, small but vicious, had introduced into Dutch political life elements of violence, terror, and intimidation hitherto unknown, and they had set out to wreck the rally weeks beforehand with classic Nazi methods. They had sent threatening anonymous letters to the speakers, mutilated the facades of their houses with slogans crudely painted with a tar brush; they had made it known to the press that if the rally were held, they would be there to throw stink bombs and set off fireworks to protest against what they termed "an unfriendly act towards a friendly nation." I don't know what happened to the others, but of the three speakers, only my father turned up.

My mother and I had tried in vain to dissuade him; our argument had been that because of the Nazi threats, the protest meeting had been lowered to the level of a brawl in which, as a man of the cloth, he had no business getting involved. It seemed a convincing argument, and we believed that it was a valid one, but he would not accept it. I was convinced that he did not realize the kind of trouble he was heading for, he just could not conceive any such thing, but as he was not to be deterred, my mother urged me to go with him as protection—whatever protection a gloomy, shifty adolescent had to offer under the circumstances.

The moment we arrived at the Bicycle Hall, we realized that there was going to be trouble. Bands of youths in black shirts roamed about, shouting slogans, brandishing placards, harassing people as they entered the building. There were insufficient police present, and street fights were erupting. Our taxi was greeted with cheers and jeers, and hastily ushered through a guarded gate to a side entrance of the building. I was allowed to accompany my father onto the stage, and given a seat on the podium among the members of the organizing committee who sat there glumly, very ill at ease, facing the colossal, jam-packed hall. Most of the people in the audience were Jews; when the Nazis inside became vociferous, the atmosphere seemed to hover on the brink of an explosion. Then my father stepped onto the rostrum. Two spotlights groped for him from the far corners of the hall and caught him in the cross beams. He was greeted by pandemonium. They cheered, they stamped, they whistled, they cursed, they scolded, they screamed, they threw things. My heart was in my throat as I saw police move in; I knew the whole thing was about to disintegrate into a free-for-all. Then my father, a silver-haired mannequin in the crossed beams of the spotlights, did something that made my blood freeze. He slowly raised his right arm in the Nazi salute.

Incredulous astonishment silenced the audience. During that moment, in that hall with seven thousand people, you could have heard a pin drop. Then he said, calmly but with a voice that rang like a bell, "This is the way the heathens salute you: 'Heil Hitler.'" My heart stood still. Then he slowly raised his left arm as well, to a gesture of benediction, and said, "But this is the way we Christians bless you: 'Heil Israel!'"

I can't describe what happened around us after that; my concern was with him. His words caused such an explosion of pent-up emotion in the audience that I had the panicky thought they would engulf him and he would vanish forever. I couldn't make out whether it was a roar of enthusiasm or of rage, but it was a seven-thousand-headed roar. He stood, his arms lifted, in the crossed beams of the spotlights; I sat, trembling, staring at him. Then I saw, in the darkness of the auditorium, struggling men being dragged away by the police.

My father stood there for quite a long time, and gradually, the vast hall fell silent once more. Then he made a speech that many of those who were there that night still remember. Even now, all these years later, I still occasionally meet strangers who say, "I heard your father speak once, long ago before the war, at a protest rally in the Bicycle Hall." I myself can't remember a word of what he said. What I remember is my pride in him. After that, I looked at him with different eyes. That night I discovered that his courage was real, and the episode became linked in my memory with the sight of him praying behind the shed in the garden. I realized for the second time that he meant what he said: To be a Christian indeed meant to be a hero, at least in his case. I might, conditioned by temperament and generation, prefer a less theatrical heroism myself; the fact remained that he had been as good as his word, and practiced what he preached.

In the taxi on the way home, he spoke some words that I do recall. When I commented on his courage, he said, "What I faced tonight was nothing, a hall full of lambs. What you and your brother will have to face is a planet full of tigers." I remember it because at that moment the aura of his courage seemed to fade somewhat. The word "tiger" was one of those theatrical words he used so often that, to us, it had lost all meaning. He called himself "a tiger of God"; he talked about "tigers in the night," tigers here, tigers there; tigers prowled and stalked through his sermons continually and somehow harmlessly, like kittens playing. I had no means of knowing that those words would one day ring in my memory like an Old Testament prophecy.

He died in 1938 of a heart condition. He was not ill for very long; there were three or four months of injections and shortness of breath and general bewilderment, and although the prognosis the doctors gave was somber, my mother refused to disclose to him the gravity of his condition, even when his feet turned black with necrosis. She warned me never to give him reason to suspect that he might be about to die; she was adamant about this. I was only too happy to join her in this deception. With my brother away, I felt there was a certain injustice in my having to face this ghastly situation alone. Like many adolescents, I was sensitive and egocentric at the same time.

He died quietly one night. He was sitting dozing beside my mother on the sofa at the foot of their four-poster; he could no longer sleep lying down. As she described it, he heaved a deep, shuddering sigh in his sleep towards dawn, and that was his last. His head on her shoulder never moved. It was only twenty-five years later that I found out the truth about that night.

As I sorted out the books after my mother's death, I

came across the family Bible. In it, she had kept a faithful record of events that had taken place during their married life: the date of their wedding, the births of their sons, the dates of their examinations, praise that was given them by their teachers or their employers. None of these entries took more than a line or two, but when it came to recording my father's death, she had filled all the remaining blank pages in the back of the Bible. In them she wrote down the truth that, at the time, she disclosed to no one. He had known all along that he was going to die; they had talked it over, and they had made their peace with it, but they had decided that I was too young to be burdened with the embarrassment of having to face my father in the knowledge that he knew he was about to die.

I had never suspected this. Had I read these pages before, I would have acted differently once she herself became fatally ill. But she never told me; it was their last secret.

TWO

AFTER MY FATHER'S DEATH, my mother came into
her own. During the thirty years of their married life,
she had been a silent, accommodating, self-effacing
woman whose only concern was to enable her man to
hearken to the voice of God. He should not be both-
ered by extraneous circumstances like the household,
the education of his children, or financial matters.
He should be allowed to concentrate on his spiritual
mission.

My father had filled my mother's existence completely. Whenever my brother and I tried to imagine
what her life might be like after his death, we saw her
as a lost and bewildered creature who would eke out
the rest of her days in shy retirement, cherishing his
memory.

She did indeed cherish his memory. Until the day she died, she talked about him as if he might return at any moment. But for the rest, we could not have been more wrong. The unassuming, retiring little woman we had known all our lives suddenly revealed, from somewhere deep inside, a core of drop-forged steel, and she rose to the challenge of widowhood with solemn, quiet purpose. She felt she had to continue his work and demonstrate the truth of his theological concept through her conduct for the rest of her life. But what she really demonstrated was their love for each other.

At that time it took nearly a month to make the voyage back to Holland from the Dutch East Indies, so my brother had not been present at the funeral. A few months later, she decided to go out there on a visit to tell my brother about his father's last days and spend some time with the family. Now war was about to break out, we both knew that, and I pleaded with her not to go, but off she went, on board a freighter, in August 1939. In May 1940 the Germans invaded Holland, severing all contact. In 1942 the Japanese invaded the

Dutch East Indies; my brother was made a prisoner of
war; my mother, together with my sister-in-law and
her children, were put into a prison camp. It was there
that her inner strength, that hitherto unsuspected power,
revealed itself. Scores of women, old and young, wrote
to me after her death to tell me how much she had
meant to them during those years. At the time I knew
nothing of this; thousands of miles away, I was involved
in my own war. It was in Southampton, England, in the
fall of 1945, that I first set eyes on her again. She was a
passenger on board an evacuation ship for women from
the camps in the Dutch East Indies.

To convey the atmosphere of our reunion to an
American reader is difficult. Maybe only the inhabitants of countries that have known enemy occupation
are able to recapture the apocalyptic feeling of the end
of a civilization that was prevalent in those days. Young,
self-confident nations like the United States had, until
the end of the twentieth century, the intuitive conviction of permanence that it could not happen to them.
We in Western Europe had that same conviction, even
as the black clouds of World War II rose menacingly

over the horizon. Those of us who witnessed it happening experienced the incredulous feeling of unreality that the citizens of Rome must have had when their city was destroyed by the barbarians, that the members of the French aristocracy must have experienced when the revolution massacred them, that the inhabitants of Hiroshima must have experienced when their city was turned from a bastion of invulnerability into a funeral pyre. This experience of having witnessed the end of a world was the questionable privilege of the Western Europeans who survived World War II and, until very recently, the reason why it would have been hard to convey to the American reader the impression the big refugee ship from the Dutch East Indies made on me.

I had known the ship before the war, as had every Dutchman. She was the flagship of the Dutch merchant fleet. I had seen her leave and arrive many times, decked with flags and gay with paper streamers, the rails lined with passengers, her aft deck crowded with Javanese servants. At that time she had been a symbol of the pride and the affluence of the Dutch colonial empire. It did not strike us as being at all incongruous that a nation of barely ten million people eking out an amphibian existence in the muddiest corner of Europe should dominate a tropical archipelago the size of a continent with a population that outnumbered them by sixty million.

When the great ship docked that morning in the harbor of Southampton, the fall of the Dutch empire was brought home to me. What had been the queen of the merchant fleet now looked like a tramp steamer. Her paint was peeling, her boats were dirty, her flag was torn. Her promenade decks that I had so often seen lined with the white rulers of the Malay Archipelago were now lined with haggard women and children, survivors of the Japanese prison camps. I went on board hesitantly, reluctant to meet the embittered faces, the emaciated bodies, the haunted eyes of the women and the febrile, brittle gaiety of the thin children, nervously playing hide-and-seek on the decks where once their fathers had strolled in pompous opulence. The experience of the hour or so I spent on board that ship affected me in a way that I only later came to realize. It took away the last remnant of my faith in empires, nations, cities, armies, and navies. I am, in this respect, a wartime casualty; whenever I hear a politician orate with well-rounded rhetoric about the invincible might of his nation, army, or party, I see the women and hear the shrill voices of the children on the promenade decks of the flagship of the Dutch merchant fleet that morning in Southampton.

I did not ask for my mother. I had, as the ship was being moored at the quayside, scanned the faces at the rail, and my heart sank; they all looked the same. They were all gray, hollow-eyed, haunted; everyone wore identical scarves and carried identical haversacks. I felt afraid to meet her; my last memory of her was of a tiny, elderly lady, immaculately dressed, exposing the delicate, porcelain fragility of her person to the hazards of a world at war in the unquestioning belief that law, order, and human decency would prevail. I had rushed to Southampton the moment I had heard she was on board. Now I was overcome by an intense reluctance to face her. Not only was I loath to confront what the devastation of our world had done to her, I myself was no longer the youth she had kissed farewell in Amsterdam in 1939. I was still young but very different from the son she had known. You cannot survive Occupation, Resistance, flight through enemy-occupied territory, and the destruction of cities from the sky without undergoing an inner change. In my case, it had found its expression in outward toughness, cynicism, and quasi-sophistication. During the past six years, I had seen morals collapse, slogans unmasked, innocence reviled, tenderness trodden underfoot, and decency and tolerance vanish from the society of men. These experiences had left me with an utter distrust of words. After watching the air crews listening with bowed heads to the Beatitudes before they bombed Berlin, after seeing the gate to the camp of Auschwitz and its motto, *Arbeit Macht Frei* ("Work Liberates"), after hearing responsible and apparently sane politicians announce that the only way to keep the peace was to go to war, I had come to the conclusion that our elders, the rulers of society, were talking deadly nonsense, whether they themselves believed what they were saying or not. This went for religious as well as political verbiage. In the field hospitals, the dugouts, the lifeboats, and on the nightmarish decks of rescue ships on the Murmansk run, slippery with frozen blood, young men like me had come to judge a chaplain, whatever his denomination, by his conduct rather than his words. We divided the Men of God into nice guys and sanctimonious bores; if we prayed occasionally under the guidance of one of the nice guys, we did so only because it made him feel better. Empirical agnostics, each one of us found himself forced to identify some kind of a new moral framework within which to spend the rest of his life, knowing full well that whatever the framework might turn out to be, it was bound to be a flimsy one, like the one it had replaced.

We were not all like this. There were a few left who clung to the old slogans of honor, integrity, decency, and firmness with tenacity. But it seemed to us that they were only clinging to a life raft after the Old

World had capsized in a sea of disillusion and suspicion. Had anyone used any of those old slogans on me at that time, my attention would have wandered after the first platitude. Words in themselves were suspect; the only thing I was still ready to accept as true was conduct. This much had been brought home to me by the uncompromising reality of war: All a man had to rely on was his own wits. On at least two occasions, I had escaped death in the nick of time by acting against the orders of a superior or the advice of experts, leaving me with a deep mistrust of authority. I had survived a clandestine crossing of the Swiss-French border under the aegis of the French Deuxième Bureau only because I had secretly prepared a plan of my own as a backup, which, in the world of the underground resistance of those days, was like preparing for the failure of the sun to rise. I had reached the Spanish side of the Pyrenees from Occupied France on my knees, one of a small handful of survivors of a convoy of twenty-three refugees massacred by the Germans, only because I had disregarded the order of our panicking commander to stay put on an exposed ledge that overlooked a mountain pass patrolled by the enemy. These and similar experiences had turned me into an utterly self-reliant survivor, and as I walked the promenade decks of the refugee ship, looking for my mother among the pathetic crowd of haggard women, most of whom were somebody's mother, I felt a growing reluctance to meet her, for I resisted the idea of uncontrollable emotion invading the foxhole of my autonomy. I had seen men commit what amounted to suicide after being unnerved by emotions such as love, friendship, or compassion. I was convinced of their reality, and in an abstract way, I still held them in high esteem; but to an independent young human male, bent on survival after a communal catastrophe, they spelled extinction. And I was by no means convinced that the catastrophe was over even though the armistice had been signed. I had a pretty fair notion that living conditions in liberated Europe were not going to be conducive to high-principled behavior on the part of those engaged in the battle for survival.

All that still linked my mother and me, after the

Horses of the Apocalypse had passed over us, was the tie of blood, the untested tenderness of filial love. I walked the decks, scanning the faces, and all at once, from a small group in a corner, came the cry "Jan!" One of those anonymous, pathetic women came hobbling towards me on crude crutches. It was my mother, all right. But, dear God, what had they done to her? She was dressed in a faded, ill-fitting cotton dress, mended with incongruous patches. She wore one of those scarves around her head that must have arrived in bales from the Red Cross. Her hair had gone white, and she had lost some of her teeth; her features, so familiar in my memory, had changed, as every woman's features on board that ship must have done. She was, like all of them, gaunt and emaciated; the only difference was that her eyes were not haunted by horror, but radiant with love.

This is not empty rhetoric. What my mother's eyes radiated as she came towards me was indeed love, and being the man I was, I assumed that it was her love for me, uniquely. I do not remember much of our first meeting other than her eyes. We must have talked about my brother, my sister-in-law, their children, and what might have happened to them—at that moment she did not know where they were, if they were alive at all; neither did I. I also remember that, for some reason not clear to me, she was allowed by officers and the nurses to requisition a private cabin for us to talk in, a cabin that looked remarkably civilized, well kept, and comfortable. I discovered only later that it had been the captain's, and I realized that whatever the war might have done to her, my mother had lost nothing of her powers of gentle persuasion. I was told later by many witnesses about the mysterious way in which she had wrapped the Japanese commandant of the prison camp around her little finger. She had—no one knew by what uncanny, gentle powers—arranged for a cease-fire between the Dutch army and the Indonesian guerrillas, who were shooting at each other underneath the beds of the lazaret in which she lay ill at the time. It was thanks to her intervention that their commanding officers agreed to organize a convoy of stretchers to be carried through the jungle to the nearest Red Cross post. Once the convoy got under way, she was given a palanquin and two bearers who carried her ceaselessly up and down the column of terrified, pain-crazed women on stretchers making its cumbersome way through the forest. In the prison camp, she had given Bible classes to Chinese children, run a hospital for the aged, taught courses in philosophy, medieval mysticism, astrology, and the history of English gardens to women on the brink of breakdown. She had even usurped powers of second sight as a civic duty by reading the palms of the desperate and lonely, telling many of them that their husbands were alive and that they would all be happily reunited. She confessed to us later that it was not so much the knowledge of having been an impostor that worried her, but the discovery afterwards that most of her predictions would come true. Later, a friend was to give us a definition of her that seemed all-inclusive: a mischievous saint.

That day, however, on board the refugee ship, all I realized was that my mother, whom I had known all my life as a fragile, vulnerable, self-effacing creature who had seemed to be able to survive only in the hothouse of a highly advanced and humane civilization, had come through the severest trial of endurance to which a person of her age could be submitted, and come through triumphantly, be it toothless, haggard, and lame, with only a patched dress, a head scarf, and a haversack to call her own. In later years, as I pieced together bit by bit the full picture of her work in the prison camp in Java, I became convinced by the sheer weight of evidence that she had done things that were downright incredible in connection with this frail, tiny woman whose shoulders ducked involuntarily whenever anyone as much as raised his voice. She had confronted desperate situations that I knew I never could have faced, not in a hundred years. When I asked her how she had managed to do all this, she answered evasively, "Oh, when you really need it, you get help."

"What help?" I asked, discouraged, because there we went again, with the Hound of Heaven baying on our traces.

"Just: help," she said. "A strength, a power, that enables you to forget about yourself."

I thought she put it cannily, aware as she was of my suspicion of religious phrases. But I could not bring myself, not even under the pressure of that irrefutable evidence, to accept the reality of the "help" she had received. It was clearly some untapped power within herself that had responded to the ultimate challenge. I could not accept that she should have received "help" from some nebulous "power" outside the confines of her own personality.

In later years, we often had conversations about God and her experience of His presence, because I knew she loved to talk about it. I remembered that in the past, when my father was still alive, nobody who came to visit our house was allowed to get away without what was called "a little spiritual talk." Even those who had only come to measure a room for wallpaper or to repair a burst pipe were subjected to a kind, gentle, but remorseless monologue about the beauty of papering walls or fixing the plumbing in the eyes of God. I shall never forget the acute mortification with which I once witnessed, wishing I were miles away, my father saying to a workman who was on his knees repairing the sidewalk in front of our house: "Brother, do you know that the work you are doing is a hymn of praise to God?" The memory of the bafflement with which the man gaped up at the speaker, with his top hat, fur-collared coat, and white mustache, still makes me feel uneasy.

After her return from Java, my mother continued my father's work by having gentle spiritual talks with a great many people. She did not go out of her way to accost them as he had done, but she was ready to ensnare them at the slightest provocation, whether they were known or unknown to her. She received an unending stream of people in her apartment at the retirement home in Amsterdam where she lived; even her sons had to make an appointment with her for a visit, as with a dentist. An unending stream of women, girls, men, young students, children, grandchildren, sat down with her on the sofa where my father had died, and talked intensely, for hours, while she sat listening to them, nodding as she used to nod during my father's sermons to show that she was listening. My brother and I had cause to suspect that her nodding did not mean she was listening at all but rather the reverse, that it was a kind of muscular mechanism set in operation the moment her thoughts began to wander. I remember one occasion when, before going to church, she was discussing with my brother where to put the bed in his new room that they were fitting out in the attic. As we entered the building, she said, "I'll have to think it over. Let's discuss it later," before sitting down between the two of us to listen to my father's sermon. She listened attentively, nodding all the time like one of those little donkeys with a weighted head. When the last "amen" had sounded, she turned to my brother and said, "What would you say if we put it against the wall opposite the fireplace? We can rearrange the bookshelves and make a nice, cozy corner for your desk right there." My brother and I looked at each other and both had the same thought: When had she thought all this out? There could be only one answer.

I don't think it really mattered whether she actually listened to the long, rambling monologues of the people who came to see her, any more than it had mattered in the case of my father's sermons. She obviously gave them comfort, or they would not have come back. The advice she gave them, which my brother and I occasionally overheard when we came for our own appointments with her, sounded surprisingly saccharine and vague to us, but it seemed to satisfy those who had come for it. My brother, though less of an agnostic than I, could not bear those little spiritual talks; he was deeply fond of my mother and very close to her, but the slightest hint on her part of wanting to engage him in one of them was rejected almost brusquely.

Both my brother and I made a success of our lives after the war, in the material sense of the word. He became the director of a large company, I a writer whose plays and books met with success. The guilty feeling that we failed her somehow in the spiritual sense made us ply her with worldly surprises beyond the call of filial duty. We arranged for her to journey to

Italy, Spain, Africa, Egypt; she sailed to America after I had moved there. Anything she cared to mention—a record player, or a radio, or the subscription to a series of concerts, or the reupholstering of her sofa—had us vying with each other to surprise her. We were without doubt inspired to do so by our devotion to her, but mixed with it was a liberal element of contrition. He and I never discussed our experiences during the war, typical of a generation who survived the less publicized aspects of the conflagration that had taken place. But we never stopped to reflect, during her lifetime, that she did exactly the same. All we learned of what she had gone through, we learned from others. Within a month after her arrival, she had slipped back into her role of frail, helpless little woman who survived only because of the care and protection of her two big, strong sons. Then, after more than twenty years of perfect health and all the trappings of an iron constitution, she fell ill once more of the mysterious ailment that had baffled so many doctors in those early days. My brother and I had been convinced that it was her way to escape for a while from our father's mastodonic devotion, so when it struck her this time, we wondered why. Did she need a vacation from all those people who still came to visit her at all hours? I was on a book tour in the Dutch West Indies at the time, and my brother, who lived in Holland, kept me informed. First by letter, then by telegram, finally by transoceanic telephone. "You'd better come over as soon as you can," I heard him say, far away, one sad night. "They'll operate on her tomorrow, but they are afraid she may not make it."

"Why now?" I asked. "What *is* it?"

"They think it's cancer—cancer of the stomach," he replied.

THREE

WHEN I ARRIVED, he met me at the airport and told me that they had operated on her but discovered that the disease was too far advanced for them to proceed further, so they had closed the incision and given her only a few more weeks to live.

I found her sitting up in bed in a small, sunny room in a Catholic hospital on the outskirts of Amsterdam, overlooking a summer garden full of birds and flowers. She seemed relaxed and happy; but for a bottle above her head with a colorless liquid dripping into a tube connected to her arm, she might have been sitting there as a carefree convalescent after a minor illness. I did not know what the bottle contained, nor even what its purpose was; I had always hated hospitals and wanted nothing to do with sickness and death.

This hospital room, however, seemed almost congenial: so sunny, so cheerful. The summer garden looked innocent and inviting; the song of the birds, the rhythmic rattling of a rake on the gravel in the distance, the gentle wind rustling in the leaves of the chestnut trees, it all gave the lie to what I had been told. But the doctor, when my brother and I went to see him after that first visit, said, "It is impossible to say exactly how long it will take. The moment will come when we will have to stop the intravenous feeding, and from then on it could be just a matter of days." My brother and I shook our heads in sorrow and commiseration, yet there was a tinge of unreality about it all, something stagy and unconvincing. The man obviously knew what he was talking about, yet it was impossible to believe that the gay, animated woman, looking so outrageously young with her pigtails in a big white bed, was doomed to die before the month was over.

"We are somewhat worried about nursing care," the doctor went on. "She will soon need round-the-clock attention, but we simply do not have the staff to give her the kind of care she is going to need. I have discussed this with your brother, and we've tried to find a private nurse, but so far we've had no luck. The shortage of nurses is terrible these days. We'll go on trying, but you may need to think about taking on some of it yourselves as a family."

"What kind of nursing, Doctor?" I asked.

"Oh, nothing very complicated," he answered. "But she's likely to start vomiting more and more frequently as time goes on, so she will need to be cleaned up almost continually. I must warn you, she's not going to have an easy time of it."

"Does she know?" I asked.

My brother shook his head. "No," he said. "The doctor and I decided not to tell her. It—er—it seemed better that way."

I remembered how, twenty years before, she had urged upon me the need not to tell my father. If he had to know, she had said, then the knowledge would come to him from within himself. So I accepted the decision with a sense of relief. It seemed so much easier to go on pretending, and it was not going to be all that difficult, that much I knew after seeing her in that sunny room with the birds singing and the rake raking and the wind whispering in the trees.

Over lunch that day, my brother, his wife, and I discussed how to go about it. He had just taken on a new job in a town sixty miles away, so he would not have much time to devote to her; neither would his wife, as they were moving house within a week or so. As I had come over especially to be with my mother, I had time on my hands, so I seemed to be the natural choice to do the amateur nursing the doctor had said she would need. The others would take over as often as they could to relieve me for a few hours, but the main burden of caring for her would rest on me. They lived close to the hospital, so I could stay with them in the room belonging to their eldest son, who was away at university.

I undertook it with a feeling of confidence. I even remember thinking that if ever I were to be as ill as she was, I hoped I would be in a hospital like this one. I wouldn't have minded lying in that bed myself for a few weeks; it seemed serene and blissful. When I told her that afternoon that I was going to help the nurses look after her, she looked at me calmly but with an odd kind of sadness. "That is very sweet of you," she said, "but I would much rather that you just come by for half an hour every day; I'd like that. You have plenty to do while you're here and you'll see, I'll be better soon and on my way home. I simply can't have you getting involved in all this, you know."

But by then my mind was made up, and with blithe ingenuousness, I overruled her objections. She went on protesting, but not for long. Presently, she closed her eyes and her voice stilled. She suddenly looked exhausted, desperately weary. She was obviously a very sick woman. I realized that her lighthearted gaiety of that morning had been an act of will, and that she had asked me to come by for just half an hour because half an hour was her limit. After that, she was completely spent. It alarmed me; for a fleeting moment I had a premonition, misty and indistinct, of what lay ahead of us.

As I sat with her that first afternoon while she dozed

fitfully, small and old on the big pillow, I watched the nurses who came in occasionally to change the bottle or the bed linens. I badly needed an example to emulate; I had no idea how to go about nursing her. I sat there in my city clothes, uneasily on the edge of an armchair, watching.

The nurses were nuns, smiling and efficient. There could be no doubt that they had taken up nursing as an active expression of their faith. But as I sat there, trying to identify with them rather than be soothed and put at ease, their jolly briskness, so comforting at first sight, became disturbing. Whenever they busied themselves around my mother, a sick little bird between the gull-like flappings of their starched white gowns, addressing her in bouncy baby language, they seemed to erase all remnants of her identity, as if refusing to acknowledge that there lay a wonderfully mature, wise, and witty old woman, moving towards the end of her life on earth. They were clearly set on turning her, by the sheer force of their jolly ministrations, into an infant, a cuddly imbecile whom they could roll in and out of swaddling clothes, put on a potty, wipe, powder, pat, tuck in, and leave behind, drowsy with contentment, sucking a comforter. Their very praise for her behavior as a patient— "Oh, isn't she sweet?" and "She's one of the darlingest old ladies on the floor, aren't you, sweetheart, aren't you?"—seemed to isolate my mother into heartbreaking loneliness, a solitary figure on an immense and empty beach, facing the awesome ocean of death.

After they had left, I sat down by her bedside and took her hand and tried to put into words the tenderness and the love, the realization of her uniqueness, her great and glorious life that I felt so urgent and so articulate within me; but the moment she opened her eyes and recognized me, she fell back, with an effort of will that was profoundly alarming, into her role of the gay convalescent with the pigtails whom she had impersonated that morning. But this time her performance did not ring true. The birds in the garden had grown silent; the gathering darkness of dusk had dulled the colors of the flowers outside; the first chill of the night had come creeping in through the open window. I realized that she would never relax in my presence if I continued to show up as a visitor for whom she had to put up a brave front. If I wanted to help her, instead of prompting her to help me, I would have to become part of her world, the world of the hospital, of sickness, fear, a shaded light in the night, shadows on the ceiling, people in white coats. I asked the matron for a white coat; as she did not have a spare, I went home to my brother's house and put on a tennis shirt and white trousers. When I came back to her that evening, she looked up and said, "Doctor . . ."

I said, "No, Mama, it's me."

"Oh," she said, bewildered; she half rose on her elbow to force herself back into that role; then she fell back wearily and said "Oh" again, but this time in a tone of acceptance.

So I started to look after her as an orderly. I improvised from minute to minute, discovering the elementary techniques of nursing as I went along, and committing elementary blunders at every turn of the road. I learned how to handle and help an inert body perform the basic functions of life, manhandling her in the most clumsy fashion, stopping us frequently in bizarre positions, dancers in a grotesque ballet frozen in midmotion, trembling on the brink of panic. Without either of us knowing of its existence, she became my "Mr. Chase"—the name given in nursing school to the man-sized doll on which the students practice basic patient care.

It was only thanks to her indomitable sense of humor that the whole thing did not disintegrate into a nightmare. Whenever I was caught in an inextricable position while trying to lift her onto the bedpan, or having her end up wrapped in a wet sheet while trying to change her bed without removing her from it, it was always her giggle that smoothed out the panic and relaxed me sufficiently to try again from the beginning. I undoubtedly hurt her more than I realized, but she bore it without complaint. At times she even seemed to prefer my clumsy bungling to the professional efficiency of the nurses and reached the point where she would say to them as they came in, "No, thank you,

that is not necessary, my son has already done that,"
whereas her son had not done anything of the sort.
After the nurses had closed the door behind them and
we were alone again, I would look at her reproachfully
and with apprehension, but she would smile and say,
"Come on, let's give it a try. Don't worry, take your
time." And I would proceed to give her a bed bath with
the zest of a three-year-old washing a car.

This went on for a week; at the end I began to endow
myself, in moments of overconfidence, with a natural
talent for nursing. I stayed with her for twelve hours
a day, with short interruptions when my sister-in-law
or one of the older children came and took over for a
while. As far as the night hours were concerned, I was
assured by the matron that help was not needed because
my mother slept straight through from ten to six thanks
to an injection given to all critical patients to ease the
workload of the night shift. As I reflected on that infor-
mation, it seemed a shade too forthright for comfort,
but at least it was honest.

That first week, despite its undertone of sadness

and farewell that ambushed us at unexpected moments, was our best. Her decline was so gradual that it was barely noticeable; she began to vomit more frequently, but we worked out a technique that seemed almost to neutralize its misery. I saw to it that there was always a clean emesis basin and a box of tissues standing by, some ice water in the jug and a freshly cut rose from my brother's garden in the vase by her bedside. As she began to retch, I helped her by cradling her head in my hand, then wiping her mouth with tissues, washing her chin, and wetting her eyes with ice water; to undo the odor that could not be washed away, I let her smell the perfume of the rose I had brought in that day. The way she drank in the scent of the flower, her eyes closed, her face harrowed and tragic with uncounted memories and associations known only to her and to God, was almost unbearable to watch. In those moments the irrevocable future seemed to be there already, in all its awesome finality, and I felt I could stand it no longer, as if my heart would break, as though I would burst into tears and break down on her emaciated body and sob with childish grief and horror, in the sudden realization that she was about to go away forever. But I always managed to catch myself in time, not by thinking of other things, I had tried that, but by focusing on and identifying with her. It always seemed to work; I did not give it much thought, but what it amounted to was that I could help her only as long as I completely forgot about myself.

Then, one morning as I came in, she received me with a face so masklike with horror, so frozen with desperate courage, that my heart sank.

"What is it?" I asked.

She gazed at me for a moment without speaking, with an awful look of pain and fear and unspeakable loneliness. "Well," she said at last, "a nurse came by a while ago and said that I should tell my next of kin to go to the office as soon as possible . . ."

I didn't know what to say. Surely not so soon . . . This was counter to all our arrangements with the doctor. I couldn't understand it. "What did she mean?" I asked lamely.

My mother shook her head, unable to answer.

It couldn't be, it couldn't be. "I—I'll go and find out," I said, and hurried from the room.

When I finally found the woman who had visited her at six o'clock that morning, I found a beaming fat nun sitting in an office behind a desk, scratching in a ledger with a pen, wearing oval-rimmed glasses. I asked her if it was she who wanted to see the next of kin of Mrs. de Hartog. She said with disarming bonhomie, "Yes, yes, indeed," rummaged among some papers in a basket marked PENDING, then handed me one, saying, "I realize that you have other things on your mind, but you should know that last week's bill is two days over-due!" I apologized with shaking knees, so outraged that all I could find to express what I felt were words of Mephistophelean courtesy. I thanked her for her for-bearance, assured her that the error would be corrected at the earliest opportunity, and left her presence back-wards, bowing.

When I returned to my mother and told her what had happened, she gazed at me, openmouthed with dis-belief, for a long motionless moment; then she burst out laughing. She laughed, laughed until the tears ran down her face and her shoulders shook; she laughed until she fell back in the pillows, exhausted. When I bent over her apprehensively, she opened her eyes and looked at me with a joy and a love that I'll never forget and said, "Please, please, don't be angry with her! Of such is the Kingdom of Heaven."

The next morning it was a different story. The chief resident called me into his office. He was grave and matter-of-fact. "I need to talk to you," he said, then he talked about the intravenous feeding and how it would have to be stopped within the next day or two. I never quite understood why, but he gave medical reasons that sounded irrefutable. Then he asked me whether I had any objection to their terminating the intravenous feeding that same day. I didn't know what to say. It seemed unfair that I should be forced to even take part in such an awesome decision. It meant, I realized, to consciously condemn her to a lingering death by starvation with no drugs to allay the discomfort. I called my brother, he talked to the doctor, and, in the end, we somehow agreed that if the intravenous feeding had to be terminated, it had better be done as soon as possible.

I was there when the nurse came to remove the needle. She did so with a cheerfulness that was to me, at that moment, profoundly disturbing. "Congratulations," she said gaily, "it can come out now, how about that?" Then she pulled it out, thereby starting the starvation from which the patient would die. My mother, so worldly-wise and so perceptive, with such immense experience and such deep knowledge of human nature, never seemed to suspect the truth. Since the incident of "the next of kin" the day before, she seemed a changed woman. For the first time since she had entered the hospital, she seemed convinced that she would leave it cured.

I don't know how I bore up under this. My show of calm equanimity cannot have been very convincing, but she seemed unaware of any signs of strain.

That afternoon a young surgeon came by with a nurse to inspect the incision and to inquire after her well-being. I sat there, steeped in sorrow and gloom as he came in, tanned from the beach, double-chinned at thirty, in a crackling, starched white coat, smelling of aftershave. I felt a juvenile animosity towards him when, after glancing at the incision, he said with virile heartiness, "Well, the stitches can come out now! Good show!" To the nurse, he said, "She is allowed liquids now, and you can increase that gradually." Then he left. I wondered whether he realized that any liquids she took by mouth came back within no time at all, and what a ludicrous thing it would be to increase that. At that moment I had a poor opinion of the medical profession.

The week that followed was a nightmare. The removal of the IV needle had been the beginning of the end, and the end came slowly, with spine-chilling relentlessness. Anyone who doubts that there is a power of evil afoot in this universe need only be present at the lingering death of a patient afflicted with my mother's disease, if treated the way she was treated. Even the Gestapo in its heyday could not have thought of variations of torture with more diabolical inventiveness. It started with an accelerated increase of the times she vomited during the day, and what she brought up was not something taken by mouth. It marked the beginning of a mounting horror that I battled with in mounting panic as with a dark angel of death. The faint, nauseating smell that we had tried to combat with the scent of a rose grew into an indescribable stench of putrefaction. It seemed an emanation of corruption, of rabid suicidal evil, of the demon cancer killing itself in a blaze of obscene triumphant self-destruction. But all these are words; I cannot describe that odor. It defeated everything in me that wanted to help, to love, to succor. I tried to escape from it, I tried to get it out of my nostrils by rubbing leaves and inhaling their perfume, like a village idiot in dark lanes at night. I fled to the bus station that had often nauseated me with its malodorous combination of diesel and smoke, but to no avail. I drank Dutch gin and French wine, sucked peppermints, ate spicy food, cleaned out my nostrils with eau de cologne; I could not chase it. It haunted me wherever I went; it choked me in my sleep with the groping tentacles of nightmares. To return to her in the morning became more and more of a battle. I would stand for minutes outside her door with my hand on the knob, trying to conjure up the strength to go in there and face with a smile the pointless, cruel, obscene destruction of this little body, this great spirit, this wonderful, wonderful woman.

My brother gave up before I did; in a way, he was more honest with himself. One afternoon after we had fled together from her presence under the pretext that he had to show me something in his car, he told me that he could no longer bear to watch her go through that torment. Throughout his life, he said, he had confidently left the decisions about religion to those experts who devoted their lives to its contemplation. What he now saw happening in front of his eyes convinced him that there could be no God, at least no God of love; for why should a saintly woman who had never done anybody any harm die like that, like a dog driven over by a mowing machine, whereas a business acquaintance of his, a stupid, greedy reprobate, had been allowed to die *in flagrante?* I had no answers for him. All I had was a waning reserve of love that drew me back to her bedside in powerless devotion. But that night she went mad.

Back in my nephew's room at the house, it was impossible to sleep, so finally I got up, dressed, and went for a short walk. As I passed the hospital, on impulse I decided to drop by to check on her. Earlier that evening, the nurse coming on duty had reassured me yet again that my mother would be perfectly all right during the hours of darkness, the injection always gave her a good night's sleep. "Get some rest yourself, Mr. de Hartog, you need it. Take it easy tomorrow morning, there is no need for you to come in until after nine. The day shift will bathe her when they come on." She had sounded calm, confident, detached. Very detached—she always referred to the dying with an indulgent smile as "they." "They" usually started to pluck at their bedclothes as the end approached. "They" usually became naughty at times, trying to climb out of bed or tear their nighties. "They" were usually restless when darkness fell, but calmed down after the injection.

I had inquired whether "they" remained conscious until the very end, realizing, even as I asked it, that in a puerile effort to appear manly and objective, I had called my mother "they." It was as if I had surrendered her to that other world, the twilight world of horror and nightmare and utter loneliness, the world of the damned.

Maybe that was why I went back to see her that night; maybe it was just chance. As I entered the hospital, which seemed silent and deserted, and approached her door with the green light over it that meant "critical patient," I heard a sound that made my blood freeze. It was a low, growling, bestial sound, followed by a sharp rattling, as of the gate to a cage being rattled by an enraged animal in the zoo. My first thought was that a psychiatric patient had broken loose and found his way into her room; when I threw open the door and stood on the threshold, I found her standing up in her bed. But it was no longer her bed; the side rails had been pulled up to prevent her from falling out, her wrists had been restrained by straps tied to the bed frame, and there she stood, shaking, growling, with bloodshot eyes, her sweat-soaked hair matted on her forehead, her soiled nightgown torn to shreds. As I stood there in inexpressible horror and grief and panic, I knew that I could not face this. For the first time, I broke and cried, "Nurse! Nurse! Nurse!" and two of them came running. I stayed outside; I could not go in and I could not leave; I heard them struggle with that demon inside and I heard her voice scream out, "Leave me alone with your stupid injections! Get out, both of you! Oh God, dear God, help me, help me, I cannot wander about this town any longer . . ."

When at last it became silent, I opened the door and looked in. She lay, panting, on her back in the tangle of her bedclothes; one of the nurses was removing the needle. The day's rose that she had sniffed after each little ritual of cleaning up lay trampled on the floor. Her Bible had fallen off the nightstand and shed ribbons, dried flowers, yellowed snapshots of people long dead. I wanted to go to her; then she started to retch. The stench was such that I reeled back and fled from the room.

Presently, as I sat outside in the corridor on a chair against the wall, one of the nurses patted my shoulder and said, "Come on, you must go home now. She'll be all right for the rest of the night. Come, I'll give you a sleeping pill, it'll help you get a good night's rest. You can't keep this up, you know, the rate you've been going. Come on, come with me." I went with her to the nurses' station, was given a couple of sleeping pills, and went back into the night, back to my brother's house and the room under the eaves, where the birds rustled under the roof tiles and where, through the small window turning blue in the dawn, the first song of the new day would sound, jubilant and very loud, as a thrush settled out there on the edge of the gutter to greet the rising sun. But there were still many hours to go. The house was silent and dark; the dog in the dark kitchen growled when I came in, then caught my scent; I heard the soft thud of its tail hitting the floor. I filled a glass of water at the sink and drank down the pills, then I went upstairs on tiptoe and turned on the light in my room. College pennants, hockey stick, type-writer, colored prints of airplanes, dusty crane made with an Erector Set, first pinups on the wall—another limbo, the twilight limbo of the dawn of life, the lonely years between childhood and manhood. I undressed again, turned off the light, and went to bed.

When I woke up from a deep, drugged sleep, it was still dark. I woke because I knew, as clearly as if I had heard her call in the darkness, that she needed me. I looked at my watch and saw that I had slept for less than an hour. I tried to reason away that sense of urgency, that certainty that she had called out to me in the night. I told myself that it was a nightmare, that I had felt this because of all that had gone before, but I was wide awake now and could not go back to sleep. I just had to go, I knew it, but as I swung my legs out of bed and sat gazing about me groggily in the darkness, I knew at the same time, with equal certainty, that I could not do it. I did not have the strength to go out there and face her again. Not tonight, not now; it was impossible.

I got out of bed and knelt to pray; I found myself praying not for the strength to go out there and face it but for her to find the strength to see it through. Then, almost abruptly, I remembered a quotation from an old rabbi I had read recently in an anthology: *If someone comes to you for help, you shall not turn him off with pious words and kneel in prayer to recommend him to God; you shall act as if there were no God, as if there were only one person in all the world who could help him: you yourself.* I got back into bed and tried to sleep; I would be no good, not after taking those pills. I had to sleep for her sake as well as mine and wake up refreshed in the morning.

But after lying there for a few moments, again, as clear as a bell, that call. An almost physical sensation, a certain knowledge that she needed me. Oh, if only it weren't she! If only it were someone else . . . ! Clearly, the true reason for my inability to go was that I was her son, in which case there was only one solution: to get rid of my own persona. If only I could really put to one side my paralyzing, abject fear and identify with her completely, maybe then I could find the strength to go to her. I had already made that discovery once; now it was going to take more than a change of clothes. But how? How could I rid myself of my identity to the point where all that was left of me was my identification with her suffering? I stared into the darkness, at a loss; then, smiling nervously at my own theatrics, got up and emptied my pockets of everything that defined me as an individual: my wallet, my anti-indigestion pills, my passport, my driver's license, and, finally, the letters from Marjorie, my fiancée, that I had been carrying with me through all these days and nights. As I stripped myself of my identity, I had a curious sensation, as if something else were taking its place. It may have been a romantic delusion, but as I put on my white clothes with only my car key in my pocket, it seemed as if a quiet strength, a lightness, found its way into the hollow emptiness of fear within me, a sense of clarity of purpose that grew as I drove to the hospital. It stayed with me until I arrived at her room. But it left me completely when I heard, inside, her moaning voice crying, "Please, please, somebody, please . . ."

I could not go in, I could not, I knew I would be unable to face it, I knew I would be unable to stand that terrible odor, I knew I would give up the moment I opened that door. I had to find strength somewhere outside myself. Turning, I walked back down the corridor. I knew there was a chapel in the hospital that was open all night, and found it after a passing nurse had given me directions. As I entered and knelt in a pew in the semidarkness and bent my head to pray, there was a loud noise of boots tramping down the aisle, the clatter of a rosary like prison keys, and a hand slammed a book down in front of me. I had never before worshipped in a Catholic church; this must be the nun on duty who was providing me with the tools for communication with God. I felt like an interloper; after a minimum interval for the sake of decency, I got up and went back up the aisle. Before leaving the chapel, I turned around and made a halfhearted obeisance as I thought I had seen Catholics do.

I went back to the corridor outside my mother's door. As I stood there, I again heard her voice cry out, "Please, please . . ." It was a cry of such infinite loneliness, so utterly lost in the interstellar emptiness of suffering, pain, and death, that a deep wordless mercy seemed to break through the resistance of my helplessness. It was as if the power that I had vaguely sensed on my way here, now at the end of its patience with my self-centeredness, pushed me aside and poured through me like sunlight through a window. I opened the door.

Inside, it was dark. I turned on the light and found a terrified, desperately sick old lady, stark naked, kneeling in her own excrement, her hands tied to the bars of her cage, wailing with the utter hopelessness of a wandering mind, "Help me, please, please, somebody help me." The power that had brushed me aside now seemed to completely fill the vacuum that was left. I heard myself say with quiet cheerfulness, "Hullo, Mama, I'm here." She recognized me and said, "Oh dear, oh dear, I'm in such a terrible predicament, I can't bear it any longer, I can't bear it . . ."

"What can't you bear?" I asked. But it was not I who asked: It was that strength, that mercy, that light, no longer impeded, flowing towards her.

"Oh, how can I, how can I, a good Protestant, be ill in a Catholic hospital?" she asked. "I can't bear it, I am sure they'll try to convert me, and my faith is all I have left."

That power, whatever it was, said quietly with my voice, "Come, Mama, that's not like you! Aren't you the one who always taught me that our churches may be different but that our God is the same?"

She looked in my direction, but her eyes seemed unable to focus; they roamed over me and in the air around me, and then she said with immense relief, "Oh yes, of course, yes, oh I'm so glad, yes, I'm sure that's right. I'm all right."

I said, "You are not only all right, it's wonderful that you are here. Everybody is so helpful, and they all love you so much, surely you must have noticed that."

She said, "Yes, yes," relaxing; meanwhile, I was quietly taking the ties from her wrists and removing her bedclothes, her pillow, everything soaked with the dark fluid of martyrdom. When I had finished bathing her and put a fresh gown on her and changed the bed linen, I opened the window to the garden and sat down at her bedside, her hand in mine. It was not yet daylight, but we listened to the birds greeting the dawn, and soon there were hundreds of them, singing in the summer trees, on the rooftops, outside our window, jubilant and very loud. As I sat there, motionless, I felt that peace and serenity fill her with stillness, flowing through me, as through a conduit. What was it that was using me in this way? I had no idea, and I was not going to give it a name. All I knew at that moment was that it was as real and as mysterious as the rising sun, the summer air, and the song of the birds hailing the new day.

FOUR

THAT UNEARTHLY POWER surrounded us with such tranquillity and peace that the awakening of the daily life inside the hospital struck a jarring note. First there came, after the chapel bell had called the nuns to early prayer, the sound of hurried footsteps rushing down the corridor outside. Then there came the cleaners, clattering buckets, sloshing water, singing sentimental songs, interrupted by growls as they wrung their cloths over the buckets.

Then the breakfast carts came clanking and jangling past, and finally the two day nurses turned up, brisk and efficient, to make the bed and bathe the patient. I decided to leave them to it, went outside into the garden, and sat down on a bench in the early sunlight. Nuns were strolling about in devout meditation underneath the summer trees, coursing placidly from pools of shade into lakes of light, like white sailboats, sails gently flapping in the summer breeze. The birds were singing, overhead droned a silver airplane in the dazzling blue sky; beyond the buildings of the hospital, over the rooftops and far away, sounded the subdued roar of the morning traffic. Then the image of my mother as I had found her that night superimposed itself upon this sunlit scene of summer, and I covered my face with my hands, overcome with sorrow and rebellion. I sat there with vague disjointed thoughts about the doctor who had made me an accomplice to her torture, the nurse yanking out the needle holding the thread of life, the world grinding on in blithe indifference while she lay dying, and realized, to my alarm, that my hands were trembling, my knees were shaking. It was so contrary to the spirit of what we had experienced that night, it must be a reaction. I had not slept at all that night and very little the night before; the lack of sleep was clearly beginning to catch up with me. My sister-in-law was due to come and take over for a bit and by the time she arrived, I had calmed down and drove back to the house feeling strong and joyful, radiant with that light, certain that it would sustain us until the end.

I fell asleep at once, and when I woke up a few hours later and prepared to return to the hospital, I followed the procedure of the previous day, putting nothing in my pockets that would identify me as an individual; however, this time I did not do it out of inner need, but rather as if I had discovered a ritual, a magic key to selflessness and strength. I went back to the hospital in a state of grace. But it did not last. Maybe I had not slept enough; maybe I had underestimated the emotional trauma of the night before. The nervous strain was beginning to tell, and it expressed itself in a mounting spiral of aggressiveness.

First I became irritated by the nurses, endlessly popping in and out looking for someone, startling my mother from her fitful slumbers. Then the hospital, I realized that afternoon, was very noisy. The corridors outside the door echoed continually with running footsteps, clattering carts, chattering cleaners, and clanking trolleys. The loudest noise of all was made by the boots of the nuns, who, underneath their demure and graceful skirts, seemed to be shod for mountaineering. Whenever the pious bell on their chapel in the garden called them to prayer, they heeded its call by marching down the corridor like a platoon of guards, their shoes scraping the terrazzo with screeches that made my mother duck her shoulders in her sleep the way she had done all her life whenever anyone shouted or sneezed loudly. In the end I went to the door, opened it, and cried, "Please! Please could you remember that there is someone desperately ill in here?" When I went back to my chair by her bedside, I felt myself trembling again with anger and tension.

That day I became more and more irritated by more and more people, managing somehow to feel more and more sensitive and saintly in the process. I was certain that I had, the night before, been singled out for a mystical experience amounting to a revelation; it did not occur to me that Saul, after a similar experience on the road to Damascus, had the humility to fall off his horse and remain blind for three days. When my brother came to take over towards evening and I went to his house for an early supper and some rest, I felt outraged when I found his young sons sprawled in front of the television, watching cartoons. Finally, when I felt the same outrage at seeing the dog gnaw on one of my mother's old slippers in the kitchen and caught myself threatening him with a soup ladle, I realized that I was in no fit condition to go back to the hospital that night. I needed help, some pills or a tonic that would smooth me out and pep me up at the same time; but, even more, what I needed was to talk over the previous night's experience with someone intelligent, sympathetic, and levelheaded.

One man seemed to meet all requirements: my old friend Hans, an Austrian surgeon living in Amsterdam. We had come to know each other during the Nazi occupation. He had saved many Jews from deportation to the camps by helping them simulate infectious diseases when the Nazis came to round them up. He also was the inventor of a highly ingenious operation that undid the results of circumcision, a surgical feat he had performed hundreds of times. He was not popular with his colleagues, for apart from being a foreigner with a German accent, he was also a man of uncompromising frankness that, on occasion, amounted to disconcerting tactlessness. When I had first received the news about my mother's illness, I had cabled my brother to bring him in for consultation, but by the time my cable arrived, she was already in other hands, and my friend was not the kind of colleague other surgeons would willingly call in on a case.

I phoned him at his clinic. He was about to go home for dinner and told me to come to his house. As I drove to Amsterdam, I caught myself several times in acts of hysterical rudeness towards my fellow motorists, tapping my forehead, shaking my fist, and mouthing words incongruent with the spirit of the night before. It was obviously high time I went for help.

A widower, Hans lived alone with an intimidated elderly housekeeper in a huge, somber house in the old, somber part of town. I found him having a lonely supper at the head of an empty table in the huge, empty dining room with, as his sole companion, a grandfather clock, ten feet tall, chatty with ticktocks and occasional bursts of silvery chimes. When I came in, he was gulping down some liquid dessert with the table manners of a castaway, his chin virtually in the bowl. After a cursory greeting, he continued to eat, burping and slurping as I talked.

His response was blunt and to the point. The whole thing was insane, he said; I had no business nursing my mother. I should have taken a night nurse, two night nurses, three night nurses, hell, they came a dime a dozen; anyone saying they did not was a liar. Holland was lousy with nurses: bad nurses, sure, but better nurses than I, in any case. What did I think I was doing? He didn't wait for me to tell him; he told me. It was this ghoulish Dutch tradition of trooping the family in front of a dying relative's bed, that was what it was. No wonder Dutch stiffs looked so pained and exhausted; anybody would after seeing the histrionics of fifteen distant cousins miming grief at a last image of life. It was as barbaric as that other charming Dutch custom: that the husband should be present in the room while his wife was giving birth. Where else in the civilized world would one find such obscene remnants of archaic tribal traditions?

I said, "Look, Hans, I've come to ask you for some pills, not—"

But he was at last having some company other than the grandfather clock, and he was going to get the last ounce of company out of me if it killed me. Death was a private matter, he said, the most private matter of a lifetime. Then, at last, each individual was confronted with his God. Not his Creator, mind you: the God he had created himself during his lifetime. It was a situation in which no one should interfere, certainly not the son of a woman who had been dealing in God for eighty years. Nothing I could do, or say, or pray, or think, or wash, or lug on to the bedpan could change her fate. To be executed by the hand of her own personal God, that was what life was about, that—

I said pleadingly, "Hans! I may have done everything wrong, I may be anything you say, but I started this, and I must see it through . . ."

He eyed me dourly. "Why do you have to see it through?" he asked. "You've pestered her enough with your juvenile bout of charity. Get a nurse, say goodbye to her, and—"

The grandfather clock intervened and played the national anthem. I sat listening, shaking like a leaf, as my friend gulped down the second helping of his dessert to the accompaniment of chimes. Then I began to laugh. It was either that or take the bowl and crown him with it.

He ignored my emotional display and asked, "How is she otherwise?" I told him about my overnight experience; he was not interested in my revelation, however. He was interested in her incongruous behavior. Did she get that agitated during the day? I shook my head. He hummed, pursed his lips, then glanced at the clock and said, "Pick up that phone and call the hospital. Tell them not to give her any sedative injections tonight."

I was stunned. "You think that was why . . . ?"

He said, "Go ahead, call them, and if they protest, tell them that there is no need for it; if necessary, you'll see she has a private nurse. You may also, if they object, point out to them that the primary need of a woman who has only a few more days to live is not sleep."

I telephoned the hospital and spoke to the head nurse of the evening shift, who said that the injection could be canceled only on doctor's orders. I called the doctor, who was sympathetic but obviously did not appreciate my interference in what was, after all, his province. He promised, however, that he would call the hospital and cancel the injection. Once I had put down the receiver, I asked if it could indeed be that her horrible hallucinations had been a result of the routine nighttime injections, which were apparently given to all patients. My friend shrugged his shoulders and said, "How can I say without having seen her? Let me get you your pills."

But he had lit a fuse that I was unable to stamp out. As I drove back to my brother's house, the thought that my mother had been dragged through the tortures of hell because of mere medical nonchalance made me clutch the wheel of my car with anger, rehearsing conversations with the medical staff.

It was obvious that I was not in a fit state to go to the hospital.

My brother took over for some hours. I swallowed two pills, and they were very effective. I had to be shaken awake four hours later, as arranged, to give him a chance to get some sleep before leaving for his office early the next morning. It was two o'clock at night.

I dressed as before and went to the hospital, telling myself that I had regained some of the serenity of the previous night; but as I neared her room, I heard that horrible familiar growling in the distance, and that rattling of bars, as by a caged beast. I ran down the corridor and found my brother sitting on the chair outside her door, his eyes wide with horror, his face a motionless mask. As I went to open the door, he said, "No, no! Don't go in there. The nurses are with her. They are giving her another injection. She'll be all right in a while."

I said, "Another injection? Was she given one earlier tonight?"

"Yes, of course," he said. "You know, the one to help her sleep. I was right there with her, she fell asleep without any problem, I sat reading a book; then, about ten minutes ago, suddenly, she . . . she just went mad . . ."

I ran to the telephone and called the doctor out of his bed. When I told him what had happened, he answered that unfortunately he had not had a chance to call the hospital until late that evening because of an emergency, and had been informed that they had already given her the nightly injection. He had told them to stand by and, at the slightest sign of excitement, to give her another dose.

Speechless, I put the telephone down. Instead of feeling a radiant power of light and love within me, I felt another power, equally strong and compelling, threatening to swamp me with a blind, destructive rage. The night before, I had stretched out my hands towards my mother as in a blessing of mercy. Now I stood in that corridor with clenched fists, fighting a wild desire to wring that goddamn doctor's neck and slap that goddamn nurse's face, not once but twice, three times, four . . . ! I buried my face in my hands and moaned, "Oh God, help me, deliver me from this horror." But God, whoever or whatever He might be, did not come running. All I was granted was the knowledge that if I stayed on in the hospital, I would wreak havoc. I dared not enter that room, not then. I called Hans, told him of the situation, and asked him for the phone number of one of those nurses he had mentioned. He said he didn't have any phone numbers other than that of the surgical nurse at his clinic, and he would give her a call.

I waited in the telephone booth for him to call me back. I sat there, my eyes tightly closed, my hands over my ears, for what seemed a very long time. Then the telephone rang. "All right," he said, "she's on her way. Now leave and get off to bed. You have no business being there. Go to bed, take a couple of my pills, and sleep."

I told him that I had already taken two; he said, "So,

what the hell, take another two. Knock yourself out for twenty-four hours and give that marvelous, wonderful woman a chance to die in peace!"

I stammered, "Please, please, Hans, don't say that right now . . ."

But he was incorruptible. "No use beating about the bush," he said. "I've seen it happen too often in this country. Only when the family has the good grace to turn away, at long last, will the patient die in peace and privacy, the way she's supposed to."

I said, "Thank you."

He said, "Don't mention it. Good luck, old friend."

My brother and I drove back through the darkened streets, underneath a sky luminous with stars. We didn't say much, but when we got out of the car, we walked up to the house with our arms around each other's shoulders. We went to bed after having drunk a glass of milk in the kitchen, as we used to do at home after coming in late from the movies. We didn't say a word, but we each knew that the other was going through the same agony of memories and apprehension. We finally climbed the stairs heavy with sorrow and sadness.

After an hour of tossing and turning, I could stand it no longer. I dressed again, tiptoed out, and went back to the hospital. I wanted to see if the nurse had arrived. She had. She was sitting in a corner of the room underneath a standard lamp shaded with a towel, writing a letter. My mother, a small, still form underneath the white cover, seemed peacefully asleep. "Don't worry," the nurse whispered. "She'll be all right, I'm watching her. She's resting nicely now. See you in the morning."

She resumed writing her letter, and I went home.

We were roused a couple of hours later by the telephone. It was the nurse, calling to say that my mother had died.

FIVE

THE BODY WE FOUND laid out on the bed was so emaciated, the face, finally frozen in the stillness of death,
a mask of such unimaginable suffering, that she was
completely unrecognizable, a stranger.

As I stood looking down at her, I felt nothing. It
seemed as if all tenderness had been stunned by the
unspeakable horror of those violent nights. A numbness
had settled like a balm over my brutalized sensibility.

She was buried in the family grave in a vast, wooded
graveyard outside Amsterdam. While the casket was
lowered, I read the thirteenth chapter of Paul's first letter to the Corinthians, which she had often asked me to
read to her during the last stage of her illness. A thrush
sang in the trees behind the grave; it was still singing as
the small group of mourners slowly walked away forever.

The next day we started to dismantle her world. We sorted out her possessions in the retirement home; there were many books, rows upon dusty rows of them arranged on shelves in the corridors of the home and crates upon crates in the attic. Most of these made up our father's theological and philosophical library, eventually sold to a Christian bookseller from the provinces. He bought the Schopenhauer and Nietzsche Lecture Series and Calvin's writings by weight. He was not interested in our mother's small library, consisting of a few score of esoteric books on mysticism with forbidding titles like *The Cloud of Unknowing, The Ancren Riwle, Sayings of Rabbi Aaron Leib of Primishlan, Disciple of the Maggid of Zlotchov.* He advised us to donate these, together with our father's dog-eared detective novels, to the Salvation Army, which would sell them for pulp. This we hesitated to do. Surely, we thought, there must be a group of people, somewhere in Holland, interested in mysticism. Maybe those people called Quakers whose meetings she sometimes attended, weren't they some kind of mystical sect? I looked them up in the Amsterdam phone book, found "Quaker Centrum"; a woman's voice answered. They would send someone to look at the books.

The next day a middle-aged lady turned up, introducing herself as their librarian. She wore a hirsute tweed suit and sensible shoes suggestive of a propensity for health foods; she had brought a shopping basket to take the books home in. But after she had gone through my mother's library and selected the volumes she thought her group could use, her basket turned out to be too small. Not only would she need help to move the books, she also worried aloud about where to put them in their meeting room, whereupon we offered her one of the bookcases, at which she seemed pleased and relieved. She invited me to join them in meeting for worship, any Sunday morning at ten-thirty. They all remembered Mrs. de Hartog very well, she said; her books would be put up behind the stove, and in that way she would, in a sense, join the circle. I did not quite understand what she meant, but it obviously was a kindly thought.

The next day, after the bookseller and the Quakers had left and most of the furniture was gone, I sat on a crate in the empty room, waiting for the removal men to come once more and take away the last of her world. It was then that, leafing through my parents' family Bible, I came upon the handwritten pages in the back and discovered how she and my father had decided that I was too young to be burdened with the embarrassment of facing a man who knew he was about to die.

It was a harrowing discovery. Suddenly, it seemed that I had done everything wrong. I never should have agreed to keep the truth about her condition from her; I never should have attempted to nurse her myself. The only time I had been any good to her at all was that one unearthly night, but even that had now gone sour in my memory; all it had been was autosuggestion in a state of exhaustion, a rallying of some emergency power within me, some atavistic reserve of strength dating back to the origin of our species. Under the circumstances, my parents' moving and tender secret, instead of filling me with love for them, filled me with despair.

I went to visit the grave. Her flowers lay wilting on the slab bearing my father's name that had been replaced over the vault. The thrush sang loudly in the willows; in the distance, a rake rattled on a gravel path. It seemed as if nothing had changed, as if she had never been. How could a real person, unique, irreplaceable, loving, alive, vanish without a trace, forever? Where was she? Where was she? The bird sang, the rake raked, an airplane droned overhead in the pale blue sky. Wherever she was, she was not here.

The idea of my mother's books being somehow part of a circle stayed with me that week. When Sunday morning came, I decided to go and have a look for myself. Marjorie, who had joined me from overseas, came with me.

I had not quite known what to expect of the Quaker Centrum. I had not expected it to be housed in a small apartment on the third floor of a private house near the park. By the time we found it, we were on the late side. The street door was ajar, with a little leather cushion attached to the handle to prevent it from banging; we climbed two steep flights of stairs, a characteristic feature of old Amsterdam houses. At the top we were met by another kind, middle-aged lady in tweeds who welcomed us with a smile. I said heartily, "Good morning! I am Jan de Hartog. You may remember we sent you those books of my mother's, and we were invited to join you this morning." I started to introduce Marjorie, but the kind lady, still with that warm, welcoming smile, closed both eyes, and I realized that my voice was much too loud. She answered in a whisper, "How nice of you to come. This way, please."

Chastened, I tiptoed in creaking shoes across the squeaking linoleum of the landing towards the door she had indicated. It was open; as we entered, we found a suite of rooms, one overlooking the park, the other the back gardens of the neighboring houses. The room was sparsely furnished with a dozen folding chairs grouped in a circle around a big black stove. Behind the stove, against the wall, were a few bookcases, the one with my mother's books among them.

On the chairs sat a motley group of middle-aged

and elderly individuals, eyes closed, hands folded in their laps, submerged in meditation. We joined them somewhat awkwardly, our chairs shrieking in anguish as we sat down, like obstreperous donkeys at the first hint of a load. I already felt embarrassed because of my noisy arrival, and the unholy racket of our sitting down made me feel even more self-conscious. It became worse when, in the devout silence, I heard my breakfast start to whoop and rumble inside me. The silence seemed to enlarge the surreptitious noises a hundred-fold, until I had the feeling that all those thoughtful people sitting there with their eyes closed were listening to my digestion. The memory came back to me of those suppressed sniggers we were beset with as children while saying grace, when my father's predinner tomato juice and peanuts thundered down his digestive tract; after a while, he would helplessly explode with laughter himself or trumpet like an elephant, and, on one occasion, slapped the table in unconvincing anger and shouted, "Now, that's enough! Let's have some devotion at this table!" It seemed a sad memory.

I gazed out the window overlooking the park. The tops of two poplars swayed gently in the wind, their foliage shimmering in the sun. "We'll put her books behind the stove, so she'll always be part of our circle." Could it be that she was here, via the unprepossessing medium of that bookcase and its contents? No; wherever she was, she was not here either, among these silent, softly breathing people. If only I could believe the rhyme I had once found scribbled on the inside of a wardrobe in wartime England when I was billeted there during the war: *There is an old belief that on some distant shore, far from despair and grief, old friends shall meet once more.* But I could not believe it. She was gone, forever.

Outside, at the back of the building somewhere nearby, a woman started to scold a child. First the sound of her angry voice rose in rapid crescendo, then came the small explosion of a smack, followed by a short incredulous silence and a howl of anguish so passionate, so suggestive of outraged injustice, that, surely, none of the silent people in the circle could continue a private train of thought. But no one seemed to notice the screams; they all went on sitting there serenely, eyes closed, hands in their laps, deep in meditation. After a vain effort to shout the howler down, the woman obviously dragged him inside. There was the loud, gangling crash of a door being slammed, a few more muted shrieks, then silence. I remembered how I myself had screamed blue murder in my childhood, fully aware of the impact on bystanders. Whenever I got into one of those paroxysms of fury, kicking, screaming, beating the floorboards with my fists, my mother had picked me up, small as she was, put me in a room by myself with a stack of old newspapers, a pair of blunt scissors, and a wastepaper basket, and told me to go ahead and cut paper until I calmed down. As I had become secretly helpless in the throes of my own fury, I grabbed this lifeline with immense relief and, sobbing and snottering with heartbreaking shuddering heaves, began to snip away at the newspapers with a vengeance, always ending up, eventually, by cutting out shapes of animals, or long rows of linked manikins, or little boats.

At the memory, my heart was swamped with sadness. Why did that sweet, gentle creature, so radiant with tenderness and love, have to be tortured so horribly? Suddenly, her illness became gruesome, unbearable to contemplate in its utter pointlessness. She had been put on the rack and tortured to death, physically and spiritually, screaming for mercy, her thin, frantic voice crying out into interstellar space for help, for mercy, pointlessly, like the whining of a gnat. I could see my brother's point. Yes, so much for the blessings of religion.

I shifted uneasily in my chair. What were these people sitting here for? How long were they going to keep it up, saying nothing, doing nothing, just sitting, eyes closed, in hypnotic silence? I stared at a big framed print hanging on the wall opposite the stove. It showed a group of Quakers from centuries ago, judging by their hats and bonnets and old-fashioned garb, probably the first group to meet in Amsterdam, sitting in a circle just as we sat that morning. The date, as I discerned after peering intently at the legend, was 1660. More than three hundred years ago. I looked around at the bent heads, the folded hands, the still faces withdrawn in meditation. Even if I did not understand what they were doing or why, there must be a sense to it; they had been sitting like this for over three centuries.

I glanced at Marjorie. She sat there quite relaxed, eyes closed, hands folded in her lap, deep in thought. I felt a pang of jealousy. It looked as though she at least was able to sit there and get something out of this silence, really experience something. How long were they going to keep this up? I glanced secretly at my watch and discovered that we had been sitting like this for more than twenty minutes. Surely it was not going to be longer than half an hour. That would be intolerable. Nobody could sit still for longer than that and remain awake.

Ten more minutes. I looked at the window with the gently waving treetops. Again I was overcome by inarticulate, inexpressible sadness. If she were anywhere at all, it was somewhere behind those waving treetops, beyond the clouds placidly drifting through the blue of the sky, rather than encased in the bookcase behind the stove.

Somewhere, on the periphery of my consciousness, a peaceable voice started speaking. I looked away from the window and saw that one of the elderly men in the circle had risen to his feet and was now talking, eyes closed, to no one in particular. I had missed his opening words; what I caught was "but I have never found a better definition than the one given by George Fox: an infinite ocean of light and love." At that, he sat down again and resumed his meditation.

Definition of what? God, probably. "An infinite ocean of light and love . . ."

Maybe it was the word "ocean" to which I, as a sailor, was particularly susceptible, maybe it was the serenity of his quiet voice, but I was overcome by a memory as vivid, as real, as if it had been triggered by a whiff of scent. I had, once again, that inexpressible feeling of being an instrument, a conduit. It lasted only a second, but it haunted me during the rest of the meeting.

When, at last, we rose, joined hands for a moment,

and started to mingle with the others in a sort of social gathering with coffee and cookies and kind words about my mother, I got hold of the old gentleman who had spoken and asked him where that quotation had come from. Why, he said, from George Fox's journal! Surely I knew about George Fox, the founder of the Quaker movement? I should, for there it was, among the very books we had donated.

He pulled out a small, uninviting volume and showed it to me. *The Journal of George Fox, 1624–1690.* I had known it by sight for decades without ever feeling tempted to open it, as little as I had felt tempted to open *The Ancren Riwle* or *The Cloud of Unknowing.* Those books had seemed a hobby of my mother's, like crewel embroidery or astrology, something she indulged in on winter evenings to put her mind on things other than my father and his joyous exuberance, her sons and their unsuitable friendships, and the perennials in the frozen garden, hazardously hibernating underneath their paper hoods. "Look," the old man said, pointing to a passage in the book, "here it is."

*I saw that there was an ocean of darkness and death,
but an infinite ocean of light and love flowed over the
ocean of darkness.*

That was it. This was exactly what I had experienced myself that one unearthly night. I looked at the bookcase and its row of faded backs, as familiar as the waves of the sea to a child who had played on the beach all his life.

"Thank you," I said. "This is very kind of you."

"Don't thank me," he replied, smiling. "These are your books."

So they were. Or so they had been. I had known of the existence of that ocean from as far back as I could remember; ever since my earliest boyhood, I had played in its breakers. And then I had woken up, far inland.

We said our goodbyes and left, and the haunting words went with me. *An infinite ocean of light and love.* I would never be able to describe more fully the essence of my parents' legacy. They had left us, by what they had been rather than what they had done or said, with a consciousness of the existence of that ocean. And now, at last, I knew where she was.

As for George Fox and the Quakers, it was clear to me that I needed to know more about them. Who were those people? What else could they tell me? Maybe they would guide me back to that ocean; maybe I would one day set out on it myself. And then, who knows, I might even sight, from afar, her lonely sail on the horizon.